IMAGES
of America

WINTER PARK
IN THE 1960s

Displays of art fill Central Park in Winter Park during the fifth annual Sidewalk Arts Festival in March 1964. The three-day gathering attracted an estimated 50,000 visitors that year, featuring artists from Central Florida and elsewhere. The event is now billed as one of the largest and most prestigious outdoor art festivals in the country. (Courtesy of the Nick White collection, used by permission of the *Orlando Sentinel*.)

ON THE COVER: Four women prepare to depart the Langford Hotel on a trip to Oxford, Mississippi, where they would participate in a four-day charm course in July 1964 at the University of Mississippi. From left to right are Pat Flesher, instructor; Cheryl Johnson, assistant; Carleen McCuiston, instructor; and Susan Howe, assistant. The Young and Beautiful Charm Camp offered training for girls ages 13 through college. (Courtesy of the Nick White collection, used by permission of the *Orlando Sentinel*.)

IMAGES
of America

WINTER PARK
IN THE 1960s

Nick White and Gary White

ARCADIA
PUBLISHING

Published by Arcadia Publishing
Charleston, South Carolina

Printed in the United States of America

Library of Congress Control Number: 2023944703

For all general information, please contact Arcadia Publishing:
Telephone 843-853-2070
Fax 843-853-0044
E-mail sales@arcadiapublishing.com

Visit us on the Internet at www.arcadiapublishing.com

*To my parents, Nick and Connie White, who brought
me into this world . . . in Winter Park.*

CONTENTS

ACKNOWLEDGMENTS

Gathering caption information for hundreds of images from the early 1960s proved a challenge, and I'm grateful for the assistance I received from a group of people deeply interested in Winter Park's history. Rachel Simmons, archivist for the Winter Park Library, reacted with enthusiasm to the project and helped with historical information, including access to telephone directories from the period. Linda Kulmann, archivist for the Winter Park History Museum, graciously answered my questions, and her answers helped me to identify subjects and avoid potential errors; she also offered welcome encouragement. Ena Heller; Bruce A. Beal, director for the Rollins Museum of Art; and Liriam Tobar, archives and digital services coordinator at Rollins College, also provided important assistance. Amy Jarvis, my editor at Arcadia Publishing, unfailingly offered prompt and courteous responses to my many questions during the production of this book. She made the process much easier than it could have been. Thanks also go to my friend Reinier Munguia for technical help with the scanning of film negatives in a now-obsolete format. Without his assistance, this project would not have been possible. I appreciate the support and enthusiasm for the book that I received from family members Connie White, Lee White, Dave White, Jon White, Mary Wheeling, Sandie Bond, and Mindy Phelps.

I want to thank the editors of the *Orlando Sentinel*, Julie Anderson and Roger Simmons, for granting permission to publish these photographs.

Finally, I am endlessly grateful to my late father, Nick White, for the example he set as a journalist and a person. Researching this project deepened my admiration for his career as a "newspaper man." All images are courtesy of the Nick White collection, used by permission of the *Orlando Sentinel*.

INTRODUCTION

Winter Park's original name, Lakeview, captured the aquatic essence that prevails in the city, as in much of Central Florida. In 1881, two of the founders rechristened the hamlet with a name signifying its status as a desirable redoubt for northerners fleeing the harshness of the colder months.

From its earliest planning, Winter Park has carried the charm of a New England town, complete with an expansive village green and a pedestrian-centered downtown lined with shops and restaurants. One of its primary streets is even called New England Avenue.

By the 1960s, Winter Park had established itself as one of Florida's most vibrant small cities. Home to a respected private institution, Rollins College, the city boasted a mixture of wealthy and cultured residents with citizens of more modest backgrounds.

The first half of the 1960s proved a momentous period for Winter Park. Those years saw the construction of a new city hall, a building still in use, and the establishment of the Sidewalk Arts Festival, now one of the state's preeminent cultural events. Construction surged, as shopping centers and apartment buildings sprang up and churches expanded with the growing population. Elected officials regularly appeared in newspaper photographs wearing hardhats or gripping shovels for ground-breaking ceremonies at planned banks, shopping malls, and even a new post office building. Such businesses as the Winter Park Telephone Company, Florida Power Corporation, and Florida Utilities had new offices built in the city.

Construction often brought the need for destruction as well. Progress led to the demolition of some city landmarks, such as the old city hall and a set of "entry gates" to Winter Park on Orange Avenue. The extension of Morse Boulevard through Central Park yielded the demolition of a decades-old train station in Central Park.

City leaders devoted great consideration to Winter Park's image as a botanical haven. The period saw the installation of new planters along Park Avenue and the creation of Fanning Memorial Garden in Central Park, a space honoring the memories of two citizens who perished in a vehicle accident. City workers enhanced the downtown area's green appeal by planting palm and oak trees, some of which still stand in their maturity.

The downtown strip of Park Avenue hosted such thriving businesses as Irvine's Sundries, the Yum Yum Shoppe, and Café del Prado, whose names generate nostalgia for residents of the era. The Colony Theater was still in operation, showing first-run films such as *Cleopatra*. The Langford Hotel, then in its prime, welcomed glamorous guests and hosted beauty pageants.

One of the city's most treasured buildings, Casa Feliz, then known as the Barbour House, designed by beloved local architect James Gamble Rogers II in the style of an Andalusian farmhouse, still occupied its original place near the shore of Lake Osceola. It has since been moved to the edge of the Winter Park Golf Course and converted into a museum and event venue.

The period saw the emergence of the Winter Park Repertory Theater, which generated excitement, though it only lasted a few years for lack of a permanent production home.

Central Park drew thousands of children for an annual Easter egg hunt. The city's parks and recreation department staged a variety of events for children, such as summer sports competitions.

An Olympic-sized swimming pool opened, providing a home for a thriving swim club, as countless children also learned to swim at Dinky Dock on Lake Virginia. The openings of the Lake Island Recreation Center and the Winter Park Youth Center expanded the range of activities available. In that period, racial integration emerged in Winter Park's recreational facilities, even as Florida's public schools remained segregated.

Winter Park experienced the reigns of two popular mayors, one of whom, Edward Gurney, soon rose to become a US representative and then a US senator. The city maintained a robust network of employees who repaired roads, planted trees, and even removed invasive weeds from lakes.

Rollins College exerted a strong presence under the leadership of Pres. Hugh McKean, hosting an annual parade downtown and drawing such commencement guests as the renowned physicist Edward Teller.

Civic organizations made prominent contributions to the city. The Winter Park Junior Chamber of Commerce in particular sponsored many local events, such as the annual Easter egg hunt in Central Park, and the Civitan Club staged the annual Winter Park Fish-A-Thon, which put cane poles in the hands of youngsters.

It was a transitional time from the relative conformity of the 1950s to the political activism and youth rebellions of the 1960s, an era when society women still wore hats and gloves, yet some students at Winter Park High School began adopting "Beatles haircuts." Photographs from the period also capture relics such as phone booths and the common practice of smoking at public events.

Nick White came to Winter Park in 1961 as a reporter and photographer for the *Orlando Sentinel*. A US Navy veteran from Jacksonville, he spent five years documenting occurrences both public and private in the city, covering government meetings and capturing photographs of children sharing their wishes with Santa Claus, performing in school plays, and competing in wheelbarrow races.

White carried his Rolleiflex camera with him throughout the city, recording black-and-white images that often appeared in the *Sentinel's* Winter Park edition, known as "the pink pages" for the tint of the newsprint. Following White's death in 2022, his son Gary White, himself a journalist based in Lakeland, sorted through thousands of negatives that Nick had retained. Gary White, who was born in Winter Park, examined online newspaper archives and consulted historical sources to compile captions for this book, intended as a tribute both to his father and to the residents of the proud and elegant city.

The main source material for the text of this book comes from archival newspapers, primarily the articles written by Nick White and the captions accompanying his photographs. Following the custom of the era, women were often identified by their married names—for example, Mrs. John Smith—and in some cases, the first names of women appearing in the images are not available.

Regrettably, mainstream newspapers in Southern states at the time devoted limited coverage to Black residents, and Winter Park's African Americans were largely relegated to a weekly "Negro Edition" inside the *Orlando Sentinel*. Nick White did capture Black residents in some of his photographs, not all of which were published in the newspaper. His images hint at a society in the early stages of full integration, including such hopeful moments as a young Black girl smilingly sitting on the knee of Santa Claus at a Winter Park bank in 1963.

One

OFFICIALS

Winter Park officials pose with license plates issued for use on their vehicles in this undated photograph. City commissioner Francis L. Jackson (left), is joined by Mayor Allen Trovillion, city manager Richard G. Simmons, and police chief Carl D. Buchanan. Trovillion served as the city's mayor from 1962 to 1967. He was later elected to the Florida House of Representatives.

City tax assessor John Boley displays a chart illustrating the duties of the office in August 1962. Boley reported that the city's tax rolls had increased nearly $13 million from 1961. He served in the position from 1960 to 1964, when he resigned to take the same position in Charleston, South Carolina. His wife, Rita, was a teacher at Lake Weston Elementary School.

Former mayor and congressman-elect Edward Gurney visits with Leslie, a girl in the Children's Home Society program, in November 1962. Joining them is Mrs. Joseph Robinson, a state board member for the organization. Gurney was supporting the Red Stocking Christmas Appeal, a fundraiser for the nonprofit group through the Winter Park Community Chest.

Mayor Gurney signs a proclamation in support of a mass chest X-ray survey being conducted in the city in 1961. A mobile X-ray unit was set up at the Eastgate shopping center. Watching Gurney are, from left to right, W.H. McCaully, Mrs. James Bennett, Mrs. Franklin B. McKechnie, Mrs. Jack Monsher, and Mrs. John Peppers.

Mrs. J. Lynn Pflug, president of the Winter Park Altrusa Club, presents a national safety certificate of excellence to Mayor Gurney in 1961. The award recognized the city's participation in a vehicle safety-check program. They are joined by, from left to right, Ethel Ann Platts, Altrusa's safety chairperson; Richard Simmons, Winter Park city manager; and police chief Carl D. Buchanan.

11

City commissioner Joseph Romita poses with a time capsule before its insertion into the cornerstone of the city hall building during its construction in 1964. The city paid for the construction of the building through a $500,000 reserve fund started by former mayor J. Lynn Pflug and continued under Mayors Ray Greene and Edward Gurney.

Lou Manley (right) presents American and Florida flags to fly at city hall during its dedication in August 1964. Travis Kilgore (left) Winter Park's director of staff services, accepts the gifts. Patrolman E.M. Hunter prepares to raise the American flag, which had flown over the US Capitol in Washington, DC, for one day.

City manager Richard Simmons locks the door to an office at the old city hall in 1963, as a sign indicates that the offices of the city manager, city clerk, and tax assessor had moved to temporary quarters in two former residences and a garage on Lyman Avenue. The original city hall, constructed in 1906, was soon demolished.

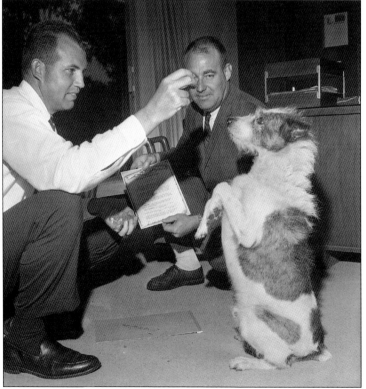

Mayor Allen Trovillion holds a treat for his dog Randy after the dog showed off his repertoire of tricks inside Trovillion's office in 1964. Trovillion was commemorating Be Kind To Animals Week in the city. Charles Crampton, vice president of the Orlando Humane Society, holds the proclamation for the week.

From left to right, Mayor Allen Trovillion, US representative
Edward Gurney (Trovillion's predecessor), and city commissioner
Frank Oliphant inspect a time capsule before its insertion into
the cornerstone of the city hall building during its dedication in
December 1963. The city asked for citizen input in deciding what
items to place in the time capsule. Items sealed into the cornerstone
included the 1890 edition of "Facts about Florida," the city's 1962
annual report, maps of Winter Park from 1938 and 1963, local
church bulletins, a sample ballot from the 1963 city election,
and a photograph of Trovillion at the dedication of the West
Side swimming pool. Former mayors G.N. Denning, R.C. Baker,
William McCaully, and Ray Greene also attended the ceremony.

Mayor Gurney (right) assists as parks and recreation director Jim Connell, center, and forester Marvin Smiley plant an oak tree in the Brookshire neighborhood in February 1962. As part of a continuous tree planting program, the parks and recreation department was installing about 20 trees a day, mostly live oaks, water oaks, and maples.

Postmaster Richard Schweizer poses in 1964 inside the main post office with Christmas cards that could not be delivered because they were not properly addressed and bore no return addresses. The post office added 14 temporary workers and shifted to a 24-hour schedule between Thanksgiving and Christmas in the early 1960s as the volume of mail increased fivefold. The office even delivered mail on Sundays and packages on Christmas Day.

16

The city commission is shown during a meeting in this undated photograph. From left to right, commissioner Francis Jackson, commissioner Joseph Romita, Mayor Allen Trovillion, commissioner Jim Blake, commissioner Frank Oliphant, and city manager Richard Simmons sit in the chamber. Two ashtrays on the table in front of the commissioners attest that smoking was a common public practice in the era.

Mayor Trovillion awaits the installation of a seat belt in his vehicle in September 1962 after buying the first in a campaign by the Winter Park Jaycees. T.G. Fuleihan (left) prepares to install the belt as Jaycees president Harry Cone watches. The organization sold 200 seat belts on the first day of a month-long campaign.

Mayor Edward Gurney delivers a symbolic key to the city to the Paulk family, visitors from Norfolk, Virginia, in February 1962. Patrolman R.W. Jones stopped the family on Highway 17-92 and told the parents that they had been declared king and queen of Winter Park for the day. The family received free meals at House of Steaks and Morrison's Imperial House.

Two

GROUND BREAKINGS AND CONSTRUCTION

Employees inspect a large gantry brought in from St. Petersburg for the building of the Sutton Place South Apartments at 500 Osceola Avenue in March 1963. The crane, capable of extending to a height of 168 feet, traveled on specially laid tracks to move across the worksite. The five-story apartment building is now a residence hall owned by Rollins College.

Crews work to build a parking lot in October 1963 at the former garden of the late Foster and Jessie Fanning at Center Street and Welbourne Avenue. First National Bank purchased the property at a public auction after the couple died in a vehicle crash. The city's parks and recreation department moved some of the Fannings' plants and shrubs to the newly created Fanning Memorial Garden in Central Park.

Workers from King Farms wrecking company begin demolition of the old city hall building in March 1963. The structure on Park Avenue had been built in 1906 at a cost of $6,000. After the demolition was complete, city officials learned that the company had not been licensed to do the work, the *Winter Park Star* reported.

Pre-cast concrete walls, used to enclose the entrance corner, arrive at the construction site of the city hall building in December 1963. A Winter Park company, Holloway Materials, fabricated the panels out of rock aggregate. The panels each weighed three tons or more. City hall officially opened in August 1964.

Construction proceeds on the Winter Park Medical Center on Lakemont Avenue in 1962. Several city officials attended the ground breaking for the $500,000 building, located across the street from Winter Park Memorial Hospital. Clifford Wright, a Winter Park architect, designed the 24,000-square-foot building, which would hold 16 suites, with a Colonial-style exterior.

City officials inspect the progress of the expansion of the Winter Park Telephone Company's dial exchange building in March 1964. From left to right are J.R. Henderson and A.E. Ludescher from the construction firm, with R.P. Hulbert, the company's executive vice president. The expansion added about 7,500 square feet to the building on New York Avenue.

Crews demolish the city's entry gates at Orange Avenue and Highway 17-92 in December 1961. The ornamental structures had stood since about 1925, the *Winter Park Star* reported. The city removed the gates as part of a landscaping and beautification program connected to the construction of the nearby Radiation Inc. building.

City officials, including Mayor Allen Trovillion (third from right with shovel), participate in a ground-breaking ceremony for Lee Plaza in July 1963. The 260,000-square-foot shopping center would include a J.M. Fields store and what was billed as the largest J.C. Penney's in the country at the time. Standing beside Trovillion is Orange County tax assessor Helen Bennett.

Unidentified officials hold shovels for a ground-breaking ceremony in October 1964 for the Park East and West Theaters, to be built at Fields Plaza at Orlando Avenue and Lee Road. It was the first time the Wometco chain had designed twin theaters. The West Theater, with 900 seats, ran first-run films, while the smaller East Theater featured foreign movies.

Postmaster Richard Schweizer (left of sign) poses with others at the ground breaking of a new main post office facility in September 1964. The facility on New York Avenue replaced the previous post office on Park Avenue. Chamber of commerce director Phil Gabler (far right) joined the ceremony, as the new building would be adjacent to the chamber's office.

Business leaders wield shovels during a ground-breaking ceremony for Aloma National Bank in 1962. The bank, located just east of the Aloma Shopping Center, opened in August 1963. Aloma National Bank later affiliated with Atlantic Bank Corporation of Jacksonville, which was in turn acquired by a bank that merged with Wells Fargo.

Mayor Allen Trovillion (left) and builder Arthur K. Reading share a shovel as they dedicate the site of a planned office building in October 1963. Arthur K. Reading Enterprises planned to construct the two-story, 227,000-square-foot structure on Morse Boulevard just west of Capen Avenue. Reading had recently bought the property from the city for $50,000.

Construction on an educational building at First Congregational Church shows progress in December 1963. The new building on Interlachen Avenue, adjacent to the church sanctuary, was part of a $325,000 expansion and modernization project. Harold A. Ward III served as chairman of the building committee, and Allen Trovillion Inc. was chosen as contractor.

The upper floor of the Sutton Place South apartments takes shape in July 1963. The 82-unit complex at 500 Osceola Avenue boasted a marina, roof garden, meeting rooms, and "two high-speed elevators," the *Winter Park Sentinel* reported. Dick Bond Associates handled rental and management for the building, now a residence hall owned by Rollins College.

Three

DOWNTOWN SCENES

A street crew secures an oak tree into an island in Park Avenue at the intersection with Lyman Avenue in February 1963. Workers cut a triangular hole in the pavement to create space for the tree to be planted in what had been a pedestrian safety zone. Park Avenue has since been redesigned with all traffic lanes east of the tree.

Parks and recreation director Bev Brown poses near a planter recently installed along Park Avenue. Behind him, some long-defunct businesses can be seen, such as Winter Park Photo and Art Supply, Winter Park Sport Shop, and Wrenn's Florsheim Shoes, at 122 Park Avenue North. Brown came to Winter Park from Daytona Beach in 1962 and left his position in 1964.

The New England Building at the corner of New England Avenue and Knowles Avenue opened in 1956. In the early 1960s, the building held Colonial Drug Store, Connecticut Mutual Life Insurance Company, and the local office of the *Orlando Sentinel-Star*. The New England Building still stands, though its exterior has been thoroughly altered.

Mark, Fore & Strike, a men's clothing store, opened in 1963 at the Proctor Centre, across from the northern end of Central Park. The 7,200-square-foot, two-story commercial building was designed by the architecture firm of Nils Schweizer and Associates. The building also housed Mister Jac's House of Beauty on the first floor and office space on the second floor.

The north end of Park Avenue contained such businesses as Frances Brewster, a women's apparel store, Rollins Press, and Elizabeth's, another ladies' clothing shop. Frances Brewster regularly provided clothing for fashion shows. Bob Keezel, the owner of Rollins Press, served as president of the Winter Park Jaycees in 1963.

The Park Mall on Park Avenue contained 14 units covering the space from 212 to 232 Park Avenue North. W. Stewart Gilman and Dan Gilman purchased the property in 1964 for approximately $156,000. The mall included offices and shops and stood next to the city's main post office until a new postal facility was built on New York Avenue.

A Christmas decoration painted by local artist Eleanor Timmerman is displayed along Park Avenue South in 1963. The tradition began years earlier with Edith Tadd Little, who commissioned 250 unique works from amateur and professional artists. Timmerman, who specialized in oils, was an award-winning painter who entered competitions in Central Florida.

A crew from Florida Power Corporation makes a repair to a utility pole in front of the Langford Hotel at the corner of Interlachen Avenue and New England Avenue. Construction of the Langford Hotel cost a reported $1 million before its much-awaited opening in 1956. The venue hosted recording artists such as Jan August and Eddie Peabody.

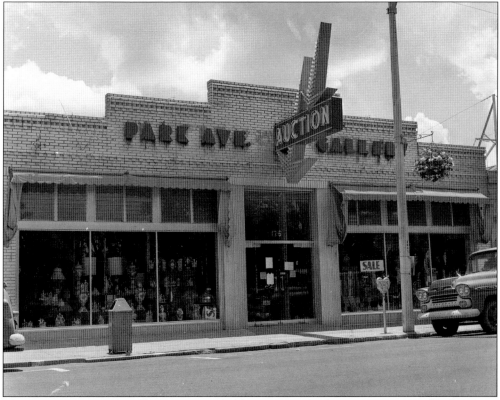

The Orange County Sheriff's Department held an auction for the entire contents of Park Avenue Gallery in 1962, and a Sarasota gallery owner purchased the lot for $5,200, the *Winter Park Star* reported. The auction drew about 200 people. The proceeds mostly went to cover unpaid rent to the landlord and overdue taxes. Owner George Shaia vanished in 1962, leaving behind unhappy creditors, the newspaper reported.

This view of Park Avenue shows the entrance to the Garden Shops and businesses in what was then known as Proctor Centre. The Rune Stone, at 328 Park Avenue North, was a purveyor of Scandinavian gifts. The owner said in a December 1965 report in the *Winter Park Star*, "Business is about the same," compared to the previous Christmas season.

Landsverk's Watch Repair was one of the businesses tucked into the Hidden Garden area on Park Avenue in the early 1960s. Next door at 324 Park Avenue North was Anne Hills Fashions. This alcove with a fountain remains an enticing place for shoppers to find seclusion or rest on a bench in the shade.

The Yum Yum Shoppe, an ice-cream parlor that opened in 1964, can be seen in this view of Proctor Centre on the east side of Park Avenue. The shop featured wood paneling and a pink parfait floor. In addition to ice cream, the Yum Yum Shoppe served sandwiches and Danish pastries.

Architect Nils Schweizer observes as workers renovate buildings along Park Avenue in October 1963. Schweizer oversaw Operation Foresight, the remodeling of structures between New England and Welbourne Avenues. The owners of Rexall Drugs and Cotterell's 5 & 10 Cent Store commissioned the renovations, yielding what the architect described as a yellow, mottled tile face below the canopy.

An informational kiosk stands near the entrance to the Hidden Garden on Park Avenue. Bob Swetman, owner of Swetman's Travel Service at 344 Park Avenue South, had the idea for the kiosk in the early 1960s to give the street more of a European flair, the *Orlando Evening Star* reported.

This view of the east side of Park Avenue shows the entrance to the Hidden Garden shops, where shoppers could find an antique shop and a beauty salon. To the left is the Barbizon, one of Winter Park's finest restaurants in the 1960s. The restaurant, which frequently hosted fashion shows and bridal luncheons, boasted seven dining areas, including the Circus Room and the Soup Tureen.

A crew paints over bricks on the exterior of the former First National Bank building at 300 Park Avenue South in July 1963. The building at the time housed the Frances I. DuPont investment firm. The renovation was part of Operation Foresight, which included improvements to Baldwin Hardware and O'Brien Pharmacy.

The *Orlando Sentinel-Star* moved its Winter Park bureau into the New England Building in the early 1960s. The staff contributed to the *Winter Park Sentinel*, an insert known as "Your Pink Edition," for the tint of its newsprint. Nick White began working as a reporter and photographer in the bureau in October 1961, following 15 months as a copyeditor on the paper's state desk in Orlando.

The 100 block of Park Avenue South is seen looking north in December 1963. Among the businesses are Park Placement, the Winter Park Sport Shop, V.H. Musselwhite Real Estate, Irvine's Sundries, Bumby Hardware, and Taylor's Pharmacy. Arthur Irvine operated Irvine's Sundries, taking over a business his parents had opened in 1922. The shop sold out-of-state newspapers and magazines and served three meals a day. As of 2023, the building at 142 Park Avenue South was occupied by Williams-Sonoma. A public pay phone with a plastic canopy, installed in 1962 in front of Irvine's Sundries, was the first in downtown Winter Park available 24 hours a day. The vehicle license tag at right displays the initial number "7," indicating that the owner lived in Orange County.

A vehicle passes the newly completed city hall building at 401 Park Avenue South in August 1964. The city paid about $500,000 for the replacement of its main government structure, using a reserve fund created under Mayor J. Lynn Pflug and continued by his successors. That allowed Winter Park to complete the construction without taking on a bond or raising taxes.

Park Avenue and Central Park are shown in this view looking north. This image captures renovations being done to the Rexall drugstore as part of Operation Foresight, a facelift for structures along Park Avenue in 1963. Architect Nils Schweizer oversaw the project, which involved such businesses as the Winderweedle, Haines, and Ward law firm and the Golden Cricket gift shop.

The Colony Theater is shown in this photograph looking north on Park Avenue. In the early 1960s, it was part of the Orlando Winter Park State Theaters and managed by Walter Colby. The theater at 329 Park Avenue South opened in 1939 and ceased operating in 1975. The building was occupied by a Pottery Barn as of 2023.

A truck carries palm trees to be planted along Park Avenue in November 1963. City crews placed the trees in front of the First National Bank building at the intersection with New England Avenue. Trees were also planted in front of the Colony Theater. The plantings followed much debate by the city commission and drew mixed reactions from residents.

The king and queen of the Rollins College Fiesta, Chip Whiting and Jane Burdick, ride in a convertible on Park Avenue in the spring event's traditional parade in March 1963. The multi-day celebration included midway rides at the Sandspur Bowl on campus and both informal and formal dances. The event raised money for a Rollins College scholarship fund.

Rollins College students arrive at the downtown train station after departing Atlantic Coast Line railcars. Atlantic Coast Line merged in 1964 with the Seaboard Air Line to become Seaboard Coast Line, a predecessor of CSX Railroad. The merger led to the elimination of the Dinky Line Railroad, which passed through the Rollins College campus.

40

Workers prepare to plant a palm tree along Park Avenue at New England Avenue in front of the First National Bank building in November 1963. First National Bank, one of the city's leading financial institutions during the era, reported about $3.4 million in deposits at the close of 1965 when W.R. Rosenfelt served as its president.

Members of the Park Avenue Merchants Association stand at the window of the Mark, Fore & Strike men's fashions store holding a sign welcoming parents of Rollins College students visiting for the annual Parents Weekend. The gathering drew more than 300 guests in 1964, with parents venturing from 25 states and two foreign countries.

Visitors gather for the fifth annual Sidewalk Arts Festival along Park Avenue in March 1964. Artists displayed their paintings and other works along the sidewalk and also in Central Park. The event drew an estimated 50,000 guests that year, and $3,500 in cash prizes were awarded in a range of categories.

The Sidewalk Arts Festival spilled over into Central Park as it quickly grew in popularity after being introduced in 1960. About half of the artists exhibiting in the early years were from outside of Central Florida, the director told the *Winter Park Star.* Student artists vied for scholarships to the Loch Haven Art Center in Orlando.

Artists exhibit their work in Central Park during the annual Sidewalk Arts Festival. The event featured more than 5,000 items on display in 1964. That year, the Florida Development Commission sent crews to shoot footage for a planned 15-minute color film that would be used to promote the state. The commission also arranged to display some of the artists' works at the New York World's Fair.

Guests peruse the works on display in front of the Yum Yum Shoppe, a beloved ice-cream parlor on Park Avenue, during the annual Sidewalk Arts Festival. In addition to the art, visitors were treated to performances by singers in a range of genres: folk, classical, jazz, and barbershop. A ballet troupe danced in Central Park at the 1965 gathering.

Children watch the parade along Park Avenue that served as a main event for the annual Rollins College Fiesta Weekend. A marching band proceeds south toward the First National Bank building on its way to the parade termination at the Sandspur Bowl on the Rollins campus. The three-day event traditionally opened with a flag football game between Rollins and another school.

The float for the Phi Mu sorority travels down Park Avenue during the parade for the annual Rollins College Fiesta. The event had an Old South theme in 1963, and students on some floats wore Civil War attire. Miss Rollins was chosen that year following a fashion show at the Gamma Phi sorority house.

The Chi Omega sorority's float in the 1964 Rollins College Fiesta parade fit the Roaring Twenties theme, presenting the Eternal Bliss Funeral Home as a front for a speakeasy. The event raised money for Rollins students in need of financial assistance. The city waived its usual $100-a-day carnival fee because of the event's philanthropic element.

The marching band from Jones High School in Orlando proceeds down Park Avenue during the annual Rollins College Fiesta. The band from the all-Black Hungerford High School in Eatonville also participated in March 1963, along with the bands from Winter Park High School and Maitland Junior High School. A field day held on campus included a sack race, a three-legged race, and a tug of war.

Parks and recreation director Bev Brown (right) stands with a memorial marker for Grace O. Edwards, the founder of the Winter Park Garden Club. The marker was one of the first installed in newly created traffic islands on East Morse Boulevard in early 1964. Joining Brown are Mrs. Holland D. Thompson, president of the North End Garden Circle, and Helen Dunrankin, the previous president.

The train platform along the west side of Central Park is seen in this undated photograph. Mayor Edward Gurney announced in 1961 that the city had negotiated an agreement with the Atlantic Coast Line Railroad to build a new passenger station. The old station was demolished to allow for the extension of Morse Boulevard through Central Park to connect with Park Avenue.

Parks and recreation director Bev Brown points to a sign for the planned Fanning Memorial Garden in Central Park. Foster Fanning owned a plumbing shop and lived with his wife, Jessie, nearby on Center Street, where they maintained a flower garden filled with roses, daisies, snapdragons, and lilies. The couple died in a vehicle crash on Christmas Day in 1962 as they returned to Winter Park after visiting relatives in Clermont.

The train station in Central Park is demolished in 1961 to make way for the extension of Morse Boulevard through the park. The brick structure had stood since 1913, when the Atlantic Coast Line Railroad opened it. After the removal of the old station, a new one was built on the west side of the park.

Physicist Edward Teller (second from left) walks beside Rollins College president Hugh McKean as part of an academic procession into Knowles Memorial Chapel in November 1961. Teller, known as "the father of the hydrogen bomb," spoke about education in the atomic age during a convocation. Teller was associate director of the Lawrence Livermore National Laboratory at the time.

From left to right, J.K. Galloway, president of the Winter Park Telephone Company, joins Mayor Allen Trovillion and Rollins College president Hugh McKean to dedicate a marker in a newly paved parking lot for the phone company along New York Avenue in April 1964. The plaque indicated the site of Larrabee House, used as the first men's dormitory for Rollins College in 1885.

Four

PUBLIC SAFETY AND SERVICES

Winter Park police captain Ray Cullifer (left) helps to corral a six-foot alligator in May 1964, with assistance from Phil Reed. The reptile had found its way from Lake Osceola into the garage of Reed's home at 870 Georgia Avenue. Cullifer said he had seen many alligators in 20 years on the force and called this one the "meanest gator I ever saw."

Cal Hancock, a fireman with the Winter Park Fire Department, performs maintenance on a pump truck engine. In 1962, the department consisted of the chief, a fire inspector, 12 full-time firefighters, and 15 volunteers. Firefighters worked 72-hour weeks, with much of their time devoted to maintaining equipment, cleaning the station, inspecting businesses for fire hazards, and conducting tours.

Cal Hancock mows the lawn of the old Winter Park Fire Department station at the corner of New York and Lyman Avenues. Hancock, who spent four years in the US Marine Corps, joined the department in 1960 after moving from Kentucky, having previously worked at the Goodyear Atomic Corporation in Ohio.

Police chief Carl D. Buchanan hands the keys to a patrol car to Sgt. John Henry Fields in February 1962. Fields became the first Black officer to be given a patrol car. Patrolman R.S. Swain (left) had been recently hired and would replace Fields on foot patrol. The photograph ran in the "Negro Edition" of the *Orlando Sentinel*.

Patrolman C.D. Buchanan Jr.—the son of the Winter Park police chief—takes fingerprints from Nancy Hill, a journalism teacher at Winter Park High School, in August 1962. The Winter Park Police Department obtained fingerprints from about 50 teachers that summer to comply with a recently passed state law.

Desk sergeant R.W. Jones of the Winter Park Police Department is shown at his desk in November 1963. Jones wears the blue uniforms that officers adopted for the winter. He joined the force in 1960 and was promoted by Chief Carl D. Buchanan from patrolman first-class to sergeant two years later.

Patrolman C.D. Buchanan Jr. (left) and F.E. Case, manager of Dodds House restaurants of Orlando, examine a safe recovered from Lake Wekiwa by the Winter Park Police Department and the Orange County Sheriff's Office in July 1962. The safe was taken from the Dobbs House snack bar at 1336 South Orlando Avenue. The authorities uncovered a juvenile theft ring, the *Winter Park Star* reported.

Patrolman C.D. Buchanan Jr. exhibits a toy cap pistol and $1,402.34 taken from a suspect in December 1963. The Winter Park Police Department charged the suspect with the robbery of an Eckerd Drug store in the Hollieanna Shopping Center. The man reportedly admitted to three other recent store robberies.

Emergency responders with the American Ambulance Company wheel a body toward an ambulance in this undated photograph. The Winter Park Police Department also responded to the call. Before 1962, the city relied on ambulance service from Orlando, often causing delayed responses to calls. Winter Park began contracting with American Ambulance Company in 1963.

Orange County deputies investigate a collision between two vehicles. The Winter Park Police Department tracked car crashes in the early 1960s. For example, the agency reported investigating 77 accidents within the city limits in May 1964, resulting in $16,636 in damages. At that point, the city had gone 167 days without a traffic fatality.

Police chief Carl D. Buchanan hands new badges to patrolmen T.E. Morgan (left) and R.W. Jones upon their promotions to the rank of sergeant in July 1962. Morgan had been with the police department for four years and Jones for two years at the time of their promotions. Buchanan was removed as chief in 1965 after 25 years with the department.

Firefighter Jack McClure installs the base station for a public works radio station, KCI-492, that began operating in July 1962. The base station, located in the Winter Park Fire Department station, used a 25-watt transmitter, enabling leaders in city hall to be in constant communication with various city department heads. It was intended to reduce traffic on the police radio.

A man observes the aftermath of a traffic crash on Pennsylvania Avenue in August 1963. The driver lost control of his vehicle, and the bumper caught a support wire for a power pole, causing it to snap about 20 feet off the ground, the *Winter Park Star* reported. The driver was taken by ambulance to a hospital.

A pair of firefighters use a rope to haul a fire hose upward at the main fire station. Hoses were hung to dry after use in fire calls to ensure longevity and dependability. Fire chief Bob Bair told the city commission in 1965 that the department needed to add the position of training officer. Bair said training was becoming more difficult because of a lack of adequate facilities.

Fire captain Ed Ballard stands beside a hook-and-ladder truck as he speaks to children from Happy House Kindergarten during their field trip to the fire station in April 1963. Student groups often visited the station, fire chief Bob Bair told the *Winter Park Star*. The fire department was then located near the train freight station, now the site of the Winter Park History Museum.

Volunteers frantically push a vehicle away from a fire as it consumes the Town & Country apartment complex in April 1964. The apartments, just south of Aloma Avenue, had only been completed seven months earlier. The 48-unit complex was on the former site of a private airport.

Fire crews battle a blaze at an apartment building. The department answered 138 fire calls in 1964, with 73 of them for residential fires and 110 non-fire emergency calls, fire chief Bob Bair reported. The city sustained nearly $1.1 million in fire damage that year. Bair joined the department in 1957 and served until his death from a heart attack in 1972.

Fire chief Bob Bair demonstrates the proper way to extinguish a grease fire by covering the pot as the Van Camp family watches. The demonstration was one of several the Winter Park Fire Department provided during an event held at Winter Park Federal Savings and Loan in conjunction with Fire Prevention Week in October 1964.

Two firefighters in full gear board an engine at the fire station before heading out on a call in 1962. Full-time firefighters earned a top salary of $350 a month in that year. The department's 15 volunteers received a flat fee of $5 for every call, according to fire chief Bob Bair.

Fire chief Bob Bair (left) and Jack Hammond of the Florida Forestry Service watch as a pump shoots water into a bog of burning muck just east of Winter Park in April 1963. The pump was capable of expelling 2,400 gallons of water per hour. The fire covered about 45 acres, creating smoke that caused respiratory problems for nearby residents.

Members of the Winter Park Fire Department use their pool table as a desk in October 1963 as they stuff city tax bills into envelopes for mailing to all property owners. The department performed the duty each year to ease the burden on the rest of the city's staff. The crew had prepared more than 7,000 tax bills for mailing in 100 hours of work.

A member of the Winter Park Fire Department watches as children explore a fire engine during an event held to commemorate Fire Prevention Week. The department staged demonstrations at different locations each October in the early 1960s to emphasize the importance of fire safety to the public. In 1965, the events included a display of a fire truck shooting 800 gallons of water a minute.

Five

LIFE AND WORSHIP

Parishioners gather for the laying of a cornerstone at the new sanctuary building for Winter Park Methodist Church in December 1963. The sanctuary, facing Interlachen Avenue, was built just north of the existing church building. Rev. Caxton Doggett, the lead pastor, and the building committee participated in the ceremony. Doggett was later reassigned to a church in Lakeland.

The Bowles family— from left to right, Jon, Rebecca, and Diantha, with their parents, Rev. and Mrs. Hubert Bowles— arrives to attend a nondenominational Thanksgiving service in the auditorium at Winter Park High School in 1963. The program, sponsored by the Winter Park Ministerial Association and the local Council of Churches, drew more than 400 people.

Members of the youth choirs of Winter Park Congregational Church rehearse before a special service in April 1963. The young women, who had sung together for 12 years, were graduating after being part of three youth choirs. From left to right are (first row) Linna Ward, Pat Seadeek, and Penny Williams; (second row) Corry Woodward and Nancy Hightower.

Arthur L. Teikmanis, senior minister at First Congregational Church, stands at the pulpit in December 1964. The church had just completed its $375,000 Building for Tomorrow expansion, which included a new educational building, an Aeolian-Skinner organ, a new altar, and a new chancel area and expanded seating in the sanctuary. The minister delivered a message of "Strength, Beauty, and Holiness" at the dedication service.

A temporary voter registration station was placed in city hall in September 1963 to accommodate those wishing to vote on Orange County's $25 million school bond issue referendum in the November election. From left to right are Reed Watts, city clerk; M.F. Moody, county registration clerk; and citizen volunteers Mr. and Mrs. Robert Gary and W.A. Jordan.

Models pose on the stairs of the Rollins College Museum of Art in September 1963. The women visited the museum in preparation for a fashion show in Orlando. The museum then occupied Holt House, the former residence of Rollins president Hamilton Holt, at 208 North Interlachen Avenue.

Sheila Clarke (center) exults after being crowned Miss Winter Park in 1963. Clarke, then a sophomore at Carson-Newman College in Tennessee, prevailed in the city beauty pageant sponsored by the Junior Chamber of Commerce (Jaycees), which awarded her a $400 college scholarship. She also received gifts from local merchants. Carol Hoffer (left) and Ruthie Edwards were the runners-up.

Eldon C. Goldman, chair of the Winter Park Draft Goldwater Committee, stands with committee members Mrs. James Locke (left) and Mrs. Carl Brunoehler in October 1963. The committed had distributed more than 750 bumper stickers and 1,000 buttons in its first month of operations and had sent a batch of signed petitions to Washington, DC, Goldman reported.

Susie Way, a contestant in the Miss Special Delivery competition, prepares to board a postal vehicle in April 1963. Winter Park hosted the annual convention for the Florida chapter of the National Association of Postmasters of the United States. The convention, which ran for five days at the Langford Hotel, drew about 350 postmasters.

Natalie Alborn Gurney was the wife of Winter Park mayor Edward Gurney. Her husband was elected to the US House of Representatives in 1962 and to the US Senate in 1968. The couple met when Edward was working as a waiter on Nantucket Island during a break from Harvard Law School. Natalie, a graduate of Vassar, had worked as a teacher. She died in 1978 at age 62.

Visiting artist Jerry Puleo works on a sketch of postmaster Richard Schweizer in April 1963. Puleo had recently opened a studio at 332 Park Avenue North, where he worked 16 hours a day. He invited anyone interested in art to visit the studio and watch him work. Puleo, who died in 1999, was esteemed for his pastel drawings.

Mrs. W.D. McCreery (left) poses with family members in her home, the historic house now known as Casa Feliz. Designed by revered architect James Gamble Rogers II in the style of an Andalusian farmhouse and built in 1932, the structure was saved from potential demolition in the early 2000s and moved about 300 yards. It now serves as a museum and event center.

Robert Bruce Barbour commissioned the house now known as Casa Feliz, designed by James Gamble Rogers II. Mrs. W.D. McCreery (back) occupied the home, then called the Barbour House, in the early 1960s. She hosted a tea for Pan American Week sponsored by the Hispanic Institute of Florida in April 1963.

Mrs. W.D. McCreery poses at what was then known as the Barbour House in April 1963. The structure, now called Casa Feliz, was built at 656 North Interlachen Avenue. The house's roofing tiles dated to the mid-18th century and had been shipped from Barcelona through Cuba, according to the *Orlando Sentinel*.

A trio from Girl Scout Troop 336 receives a check for $135.50 from Mrs. George Collins, chair of the Winter Park Junior Service League, in April 1963. The money helped cover the costs of a trip to Gainesville and Tallahassee. The Girl Scouts are, from left to right, Wendy Bennett-Alden, Laurie Harbin, and Melody Duggins.

Mrs. Emil Squillante poses with the painting *The Visitation* by Francesco de Mura, from approximately 1752, at the Rollins College Museum of Art in September 1963. She and other models were preparing for a fashion show in Orlando. The museum occupied Holt House, the former residence of Rollins College president Hamilton Holt.

Members of the Winter Park Repertory Theater transform themselves into characters for a production of *The Madwoman of Chaillot* in 1964. The troupe performed in its early years at the Winter Park Women's Club. From left to right are Yvonne Pinkerton, Lydia Dorsett, Dorothy Ellerbe, and Agnes Bower. The theater group formed in late 1963 with Walter Jensen and Phillip Dorn as producers.

Members of the Winter Park Repertory Theater pose in a rehearsal photograph for the comedy *Hands Across the Sea*. The cast included Marilyn Blake (with phone), a former television actor and later a director of many documentary films. The first meeting of the company in late 1963 drew 200 people, and the troupe staged its first productions the next year. Walter O. Jensen and Phillip Dorn served as producers.

Cast members from a production of the Winter Park Repertory Theater get into character for a publicity photo. Formed in late 1963, the troupe staged plays at the Woman's Club of Winter Park building on Interlachen Avenue. Its first season included productions of *Sorry, Wrong Number*, *The Hitch-hiker*, and *The Browning Version*. The company apparently lasted only a few years.

Six

CHILDREN

Children share their Christmas wish lists with Santa Claus during his appearance at the Winter Park Federal Savings and Loan Association in December 1963. The bank, located along New England Avenue downtown, was one of several that hosted Santa regularly during the early 1960s. Local resident Ken Wacker coordinated the jolly fellow's schedule.

A girl shares her Christmas gift wishes with Santa Claus at the Winter Park Federal Savings and Loan Association in December 1963. The photograph did not appear in the main edition of the *Winter Park Star*. The *Orlando Sentinel* published a "Negro Edition" once a week in the early 1960s, with articles and photographs dedicated to Black readers.

First-graders from Flo Smith's class at Park Avenue Elementary School take the stage for a production of *Sleeping Beauty* in June 1964. From left to right are Linda Wilson, Kim McCuller, Chris Gregory, Rosemarie Seaman, and Clay Dickinson. The school, which stood between Lyman Avenue and Comstock Avenue, was built in 1914 and closed in 1966.

Children, with some of their parents, march along Park Avenue during the annual Park Avenue Elementary School Halloween carnival in 1963. The costumes included ghosts, beatniks, clowns, princesses, ballerinas, various animals, bandits, fairies, and headless creatures. The Winter Park High School band led the four-block procession through downtown along Park Avenue.

Judy Prouse, six years old, holds her cat Sheba during a pet fair for students in the first-grade class of Frances Murrah at Park Avenue Elementary School in February 1963. Pets brought by students included dogs, cats, a caterpillar, a roach, a white mouse, a bird, a fish, turtles, "and probably a flea or two," the *Winter Park Sentinel* reported. Joanne Kennedy, a Rollins College student interning with Murrah, suggested holding the pet fair.

Children sprint into Central Park at the start of the annual Easter egg hunt in 1963, sponsored by the Winter Park Junior Chamber of Commerce. More than 10,000 candy eggs were hidden in the park, and the kids lined the sidewalk along Park Avenue until given the signal to begin searching.

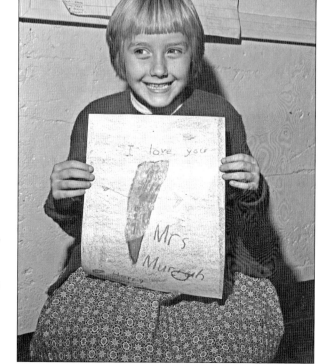

Pamela Schirer, a first-grade student at Park Avenue Elementary School, displays a Valentine's Day drawing she made for her teacher, Frances Murrah, in 1963. Students made decorations for their classrooms as well as homemade Valentine's Day cards that they mailed to their parents during a visit to the downtown post office.

Students from Park Avenue Elementary School pose while dressed as hoboes during the annual Halloween carnival in 1963. The boys are, from left to right, Ken Molton, 12; David Berkey, 9; and Allen Hult, 9. They and fellow students took part in a four-block parade along Park Avenue, walking behind the Winter Park High School band.

Children carry a greased pig during a competition at the annual Fourth of July at the Azalea Park Recreation Center. The gathering, sponsored by the Junior Chamber of Commerce, included other contests for kids. The 1962 rendition featured a skydiving exhibition and a magician's performance, culminating with a fireworks display.

Stephanie Mahan, two years old, takes on a feline appearance as a spectator during the Halloween costume parade in 1963, part of an annual carnival staged in downtown Winter Park by Park Avenue Elementary School. The Winter Park High School band led the children in a four-block stroll along Park Avenue. Some of the children were accompanied by their parents.

Sue Gipson, dressed as the Easter Bunny, greets younger children during the annual Easter egg hunt in Central Park in 1964. Some 10,000 candy eggs were placed in the park for the event, sponsored by the Junior Chamber of Commerce. The hunt drew an estimated 3,000 children, who were also entertained by a clown.

Delbert Seaman, a student at Winter Park High School, leads a class in world history during the first annual Teaching Career Day in April 1963. About 100 students seized the opportunity to stand before classes. The local chapter of Future Teachers of America sponsored the event in the hopes of encouraging students to pursue careers in education.

Fifth-graders from Brookshire Elementary School take their shots at a piñata in the form of Frosty the Snowman during a gathering in December 1963. Kevin Redmond holds the piñata aloft as D. Byrne takes a swipe at it with a stick, watched by classmates Donna Nolen and Alan Spears. The children were students in the class of Mrs. Richard O'Neil.

Members of the varsity cheerleading squad from Winter Park High School pose in the school gym in August 1963. The group hosted the Central Florida Cheerleading Clinic, one of five regional events sponsored that summer by the National Cheerleading Association. More than 300 girls from schools across Central Florida attended the clinic.

Students at the Winter Park Day Nursery play on the exercise bars during a visit by George F.B. Smith, director of the Winter Park Community Chest and a budget advisor to the nursery, in October 1963. Beatrice Richardson, a nurse and teacher, had been the nursery's director for 22 years. Shown on the bars from left to right are James Major, Thomas Williams, Dion Rainey, Nichole Harris, and Sophia Riley.

Children gather in a room after swimming at the West Side Pool in June 1963. It was the first time white and Black children had joined together at a city-owned recreational facility, the *Orlando Sentinel* reported. The West Side Pool, which opened in 1962, was operated at that time by "Negro personnel" in the city's recreation department, the newspaper reported.

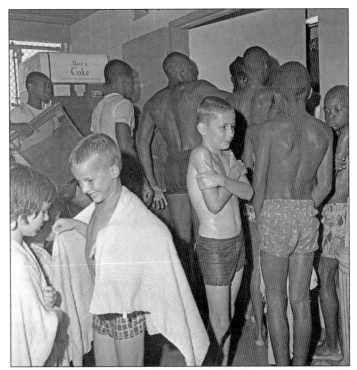

Children carrying baskets, bags, and boxes gather behind a rope along Park Avenue as they eagerly await the start of the annual Easter egg hunt in 1963. The dropping of the rope prompted a sprint into the park in search of treasure.

Children scamper through Central Park to collect candy eggs during the annual Easter egg hunt in 1963, sponsored by the Winter Park Jaycees. The organization distributed "Bunnygrams" in schools to students through fourth grade, and members scattered more than 10,000 candy eggs throughout the park. The Jaycees offered special prizes to children who found certain eggs and to

the child collecting the largest number of eggs. The event drew as many as 3,000 participants, the *Winter Park Star* reported. A local teenager appeared each year in an Easter Bunny costume, and bands from local schools provided musical accompaniment.

Children are shown with a teacher at the Winter Park Day Nursery. The nursery was founded in 1936 to care for Black children with working parents, the *Winter Park Star* reported. Located at 450 West Welbourne Avenue, the nursery had about 110 students ranging from six months to kindergartners in the early 1960s.

Children gather inside the Winter Park Library to participate in the annual Summer Show Reading Club, a promotion that drew more than 500 young readers in 1963. Shown reading are, circling the table from left, Julie de Guehery, 9; Sally Foster, 10; Karen Vine, 4; Pamela Beede, 12; and David Beede, 8.

Edgar Williams, the band director at Winter Park High School, advises students during a class. Eleven students from the school were selected for the All-State Band and Orchestra during a clinic in 1964 held in Daytona Beach under the sponsorship of the Florida Music Educators Association. Williams served as the school's band director for 34 years until his retirement in 1982.

A pair of students stand in front of Park Avenue Elementary School in February 1962. The building would soon share space with an engineering school combining students from Rollins College and the University of Florida. The building stood between Lyman and Comstock Avenues. The elementary school closed in 1966. Built in 1914, the structure was demolished in 1989, over the objections of historical preservationists.

Children from the Brookshire Heights neighborhood engage in a game of dodgeball at a local playground in July 1962. General Development Corporation developed the subdivision, which expanded in several phases. In the early 1960s, the cost of houses in the subdivision near Winter Park High School ranged from $22,000 to $28,000.

Students at Brookshire Elementary School participate in an Arbor Day event by planting a magnolia tree on campus in January 1965. Walter Boatright of the Florida Forestry Service (right) tells the students about the tree species. The teachers (at left) were identified in the *Orlando Evening Star* as Mrs. Crist and Miss Hall.

Members of Winter Park Boy Scout Troop 39 display examples of their pioneering skills in the lobby of the Winter Park Federal Savings and Loan Association in February 1964. The exhibit coincided with Boy Scout Week. From left to right, the Boy Scouts are (kneeling) John Richardson and Scott Mattos; (standing) John Greer, Ken Armstrong, and Mike Whittaker.

Students from the original group at Lake Weston Elementary School when it opened in September 1958 prepare to graduate from the school in June 1964. In addition to the 24 who attended from the first day of classes, 12 others finished after joining the school in its first year. The school had gone from one building and 400 students to three buildings and 800 students.

Members of the youth council at the Winter Park Youth Center make decorations for the annual Halloween costume ball in October 1963. From left to right are Nancy Wilkins, Ellen Arnold, Dick Talley, Daryl Spradley, Miffie Hollyday, Cinny Bliss, and Gail Green. The Youth Center occupied a location off Lakemont Avenue that is now part of the AdventHealth Winter Park campus.

Members of the Blue Royals, the dance band at Winter Park High School, rehearse in February 1963. One of the members, Barry Milstead, said the students formed the band for their own enjoyment and soon began receiving invitations to play at dances and a statewide convention of florists. Band director Edgar Williams supervised the ensemble's practices.

Seven

BUSINESSES AND BUILDINGS

A.E. Ludescher, a representative of the Winter Park Telephone Company, explains the equipment in the dial-exchange building during a tour by educators in August 1962. More than 200 teachers and other school employees visited 28 businesses in Winter Park and Orlando during the chamber of commerce's sixth annual Business-Education Appreciation Day.

Charla Johnson, daughter of W.C. Johnson, a division manager for Florida Power Corporation, tries out the receptionist's desk during an open house at the company's new Winter Park headquarters in October 1963. The murals behind her represented the company's coverage territory and the duties of its workers. The company continued to maintain an office on Park Avenue as well.

Secretaries with the Winter Park Telephone Company work with a mechanized, rotary file system called Centrac in May 1964. The system, created by Acme Visible Records Inc., provided instant access to six representatives stationed at built-in desks around the file. It was the first installation of the system south of Boston and east of the Mississippi River, the *Winter Park Star* reported.

F.R. McPherson, center, controller for the Winter Park Telephone Company, points to a service map during a visit by Malcolm Holmes (right), secretary of the Jamaican Co. Ltd. of Kingston, in September 1963. Holmes had come to study the company's automated accounting system. R.P. Hulbert (left) was executive vice president of the host company.

Robert S. Pittman, an assistant trust officer, inspects work on an addition to the Commercial Bank at Winter Park building in October 1964. The bank was installing trust offices on its second floor, adjacent to the bookkeeping department. Pittman had just joined the bank's staff that month. Commercial Bank had total resources of more than $20 million at the time.

Hundreds of local residents toured the newly opened Aloma National Bank during festivities in August 1963. The bank, at 2525 Aloma Avenue, opened with total capital of just over $1 million and 12 employees, said its president, William Edmands. Architect Earl C. Unkefer designed the 10,000-square-foot building.

Publix Super Markets founder George W. Jenkins participates in a ribbon cutting in August 1962 to open a new Publix store in the Hollieanna Shopping Center at 741 South Orlando Avenue. Hollie N. Oakley, the developer of the property, assists Jenkins in wielding the scissors. The shopping center included a Grants department store and an Eckerd Drugs store.

George F.B. Smith Jr., vice president of Security Federal Savings and Loan, joins employees in celebrating the fourth anniversary of the bank's opening in October 1963. Joining Smith from left to right are Elizabeth Slater, Margaret Jones, and Peggy Venegas. Smith soon rose to become president of the bank, which reported assets of $5.8 million the next year.

Stan Bumby works the cash register at Joseph Bumby Hardware Co., 108 Park Avenue North, in June 1963. Bumby, the grandson of the man who founded the company in 1917, had just completed a purchase of the business. Having worked as a manager of the store since 1956, Bumby renamed the store Stanley Bumby Hardware Co.

This view of Orlando Avenue (US Highway 17-92) shows an array of now-defunct businesses, including the Shorewell Motel, S&S Cafeterias, and Evans Car Supermart. The entrance to the Orange Avenue Drive-In Theater appears near a sign for the Hollieanna Shopping Center, which opened in 1962. At right can be seen a telephone booth, a relic of a vanished era.

Adelaide "Petie" Cornell stands in her store, the Towne Shop, in August 1963. The store opened in 1947 at a different location on Park Avenue and had just moved into the space of the former Park Avenue Gallery. The expanded version of the store specialized in clothing for children from infants to teenagers.

Jo Roberts Jr. (right), an IBM representative, holds a "deck of cards" component intended to replace a panel of complex wiring in a new computer system at General Guaranty Insurance Co. in August 1963. William J. Glenos, manager of the company's data processing department, displays a programming panel that had been used with the computers.

A funeral cluster is displayed on the door to the Winter Park Telephone Company building a day after the assassination of Pres. John F. Kennedy on Nov. 22, 1963. Many other businesses in Winter Park posted such displays to signify the period of mourning. Joint memorial services were held at First Congregational Church and Winter Park Presbyterian Church.

The Mary Lee Depugh Nursing Home, at 550 West Morse Boulevard, served the city's Black residents in the 1960s. The Depugh Home, operated by Selena J. Brooks, had 35 residents in 1965. The nursing home began in the 1930s as an outreach of the Benevolent Woman's Club and still exists as the Gardens at Depugh.

A.G. Bush, chairman of the Board of the Commercial Bank at Winter Park, holds a statement concerning a stock dividend declared at a special stockholders' meeting in June 1963. He is joined by Malcolm Clayton, the bank's director, and E.G. Banks, the bank's president. Bush donated $800,000 to Rollins College in 1965, a year before his death.

Members of the Aloma National Bank staff pose with stuffed animals and camping equipment on display in the bank's lobby in November 1963. From left to right are William Edmands (president), Phyllis Spencer, Ethyl Jones (in the driver's seat), Nancy Heinzen, and Jessie L. McKee. The mammals and birds on display were the handiwork of L.H. Weise, a taxidermist.

E.G. "Jerry" Banks (right), outgoing president of the Winter Park Chamber of Commerce, stands with his successor, Ken Pelouqin, at the group's 77th annual banquet in December 1964. Banks, president of the Commercial Bank of Winter Park, had served for two terms. Peloquin was a corporate secretary for the Winter Park Telephone Company. Banks said his chief accomplishment had been the acquisition of a new headquarters.

Leon Calderone and John Mauro pose with merchandise at the Wig Shop, which opened in June 1964 at 234 Park Avenue North. The recent transplants from Brooklyn, New York, offered wigs ranging in price from $149.95 to $449.95. The owners said they discovered Winter Park while visiting family members in Orlando "and fell in love with it here."

The Barbour House, now known as Casa Feliz, is shown in its original location at 656 North Interlachen Avenue. Famed architect James Gamble Rogers II designed the home, built in 1932 for Robert Bruce Barbour. The structure was spared potential demolition in the early 2000s and moved about 300 yards west. It now serves as a museum and event center.

Florida Power Corporation opened a new Winter Park office at 1150 South Orange Avenue in 1963. The company chose Winter Park as its headquarters in 1944, and continued to operate an office at 510 Park Avenue South. The new building had a window-free design, which allowed the use of the latest technology in lighting and air conditioning.

Security Federal Savings and Loan Association opened a 7,800-square-foot building in 1963 at 450 South Orlando Avenue, between Comstock and Harmon Avenues. The bank had been leasing a building at 919 West Fairbanks Avenue since opening in 1959. It reported assets of more than $5 million in 1963. Congressman Edward Gurney and Mayor Allen Trovillion attended a ribbon-cutting ceremony.

Florida Utilities manager Loyd King (right) and assistant manager George Martin stand in front of the newly opened office at 161 West Canton Avenue in October 1963. Florida Utilities, a division of General Water Works Corp., had occupied rented space on Park Avenue for the previous 20 years. The company operated five wells in the Winter Park area and pumped about six million gallons a day.

The Woman's Club of Winter Park at 419 South Interlachen Avenue is seen in 1964. The building, originally the home of Helen Morse and known as Osceola Lodge, held the first meeting of the club in 1915. The club's Civic Affairs Committee hosted luncheon seminars with prominent speakers in the early 1960s.

Eight

WORKERS

City workers plant a podocarpus tree in front of Colonial Drugs in the New England Building in early 1964. The city commission held a vigorous debate for weeks over whether to plant sabal palms or podocarpus trees along downtown streets for a beautification project. A city hall insider said the experience taught the commissioners to "make a decision and stick to it," the *Winter Park Star* reported.

Officers of the Orlando–Winter Park National Secretaries Association gather in a photograph from June 1963. From left to right are Mildred Kennedy, the new president of the local chapter and a secretary at Consolidated Electrodynamics Corp.; Ruby Eethlefsen, outgoing president and secretary to the president of the Winter Park Telephone Company; and Anne Ramsey, division secretary and secretary to the president of Rollins College.

Workers unload furniture and office equipment from a delivery truck at the newly built city hall in July 1964. Contractor Jack Jennings had completed construction of the structure months earlier, the *Winter Park Sentinel* reported, but the building sat idle as officials awaited the delivery of furnishings and the completion of interior decorations.

Workers for the Winter Park Telephone Company repair phone lines after they were accidentally cut by construction equipment on Maitland Avenue in January 1964. The incident interrupted phone service for businesses along Morse Boulevard, and it took the crew 10 hours to restore service. Maitland Avenue was being paved and a 66-inch storm drainage pipe was being installed.

A crew from the city's engineering department installs a drainage pipe in Ward Park in September 1962 in an attempt to keep a service road from washing out. City engineer Stuart Johnson said his department was undertaking other efforts to improve the marshy conditions in the park east of downtown.

101

Winter Park city commissioner Jim Blake speaks to employees with the sanitation department's trash collection unit in September 1964. Blake told the employees that they did "a tremendous job" in collecting an increased volume of debris caused by winds from the fringes of two recent storms, Hurricanes Cleo and Dora. Blake thanked the crew for the extra hours they had worked, and read a letter of praise from a private citizen, the *Winter Park Star* reported. Robert Elrod served as director of the sanitation department in the early 1960s. He left the city in 1964 to take a position with the Central and Southern Florida Flood Control District.

Employees with the parks and recreation department use a custom-made rake mounted on the front of a boat to harvest floating weeds for removal from an unidentified lake in August 1963. Workers gathered weeds on the rake and pushed them toward shore, where they used pitchforks to remove the vegetation and deposit it on the bank for collection by another crew.

Supervisors and city employees lay a ceremonial brick during a road project in this photograph from the early 1960s. About 25 percent of streets within Winter Park have brick surfaces, according to a news report, and in the early 2000s, the city allowed residents to request brick surfaces for asphalt streets or formerly brick streets covered with asphalt.

Lynda Bridgers, a secretary at Commercial Bank, earned a place on a team of swimmers and divers who toured South Africa in 1964. Bridgers was a former Miss Winter Park and a graduate of Rollins College. She had performed in water shows at the Langford Hotel, including one attended by Florida governor LeRoy Collins.

City employee Carol Alexander types notices to be mailed to residents in December 1962. The city was preparing to send out renewals of more than 1,000 boat licenses. City clerk Reed Watts offered a reminder that licenses for boats and dog ownership needed to be renewed by the end of the year.

City employee Thomas Coyle paints a sign for Mead Garden Park in July 1963. He was featured in an article published in the *Winter Park Star* exploring what the parks and recreation staff did on rainy summer days. Parks and recreation director Bev Brown said he had a list of "rainy day" tasks for his employees.

Garner Padgett, an employee in the parks and recreation department, sharpens spades in July 1963. Jake Thompson, supervisor of the city's parks crew, said workers took on such tasks as inventorying tools, potting plants, and cleaning the tool shed on stormy days when they could not work outside. The department had a staff of about 20 at the time.

Clarence MacConnel (right), an employee with the parks and recreation department, gets assistance from parks and recreation director Bev Brown in removing an air layer from a plant in a greenhouse at Mead Garden Park in September 1963. MacConnel placed a pot around the stalk of a plant, causing roots to form, and then cut off the top to be planted.

Members of the sanitation department model their new blue uniforms in January 1964. Robert Elrod (left), the director of the department, opted to introduce uniforms for the workers, who were required to pay half the cost of the outfits. Standing with Elrod are, from left to right, John Hagans, Nathanial Mayo, and Raymond Haynes.

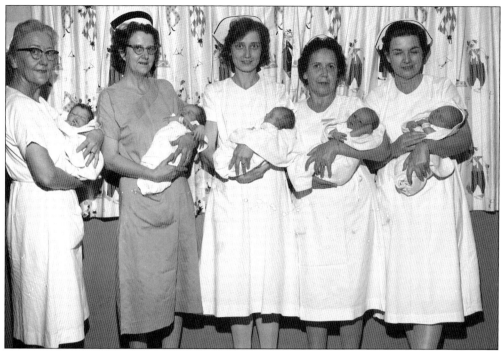

Nurses at Winter Park Memorial Hospital hold five babies born on Christmas Day in 1963. The nurses are, from left to right, Heisel Carter, Ocie Price, Rosemary Thompson, Nancy Caycee, and Nancy Schmidt. The hospital opened on Lakemont Avenue in 1955, and the expanded version is now known as AdventHealth Winter Park.

Crews from the parks and recreation department repair bleachers at Ward Park in preparation for a Fourth of July gathering in 1963 sponsored by the Junior Chamber of Commerce. From left to right are Allen McEvers, Ed Totman, Wayne Catledge, and Thomas Doyle. The Fourth of July festivities at Ward Park included a "mate-calling contest," a sewing contest, and a log-sawing contest.

Bob Lee (left) receives a service pin from parks and recreation director Bev Brown in June 1964 to honor Lee's 10 years as a city employee. Lee served as the caretaker of the Palm Cemetery. The cemetery, at the corner of Webster and New York Avenues, has been in continuous operation since 1906.

City workers conduct a repair along Fairbanks Avenue. In the background is Harper's Tavern, which operated from 1932 until 1996, when a fire destroyed the building at 565 Fairbanks Avenue. The bar shared space with an upscale French restaurant, Le Cordon Bleu. The structure opened in 1927 as a feed store.

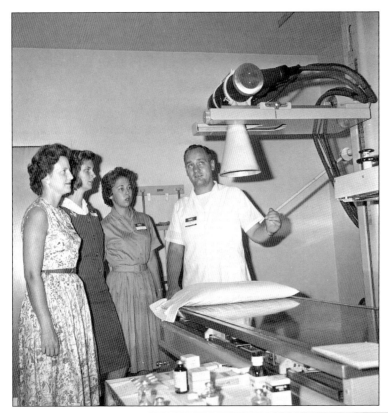

Richard Lippert, chief X-ray technician at Winter Park Memorial Hospital, provides a tour of his department during a Business-Education Day in August 1962 for visiting teachers (from left to right) Flora Ann Dean, Nancy Bedford, and Mary Whildon. More than 200 teachers and other school employees toured 28 businesses in the sixth annual event, sponsored by the Winter Park Chamber of Commerce.

Mary Estes, director of nursing at Winter Park Memorial Hospital, operates a machine used to conduct an electroencephalograph (EEG) on a patient in January 1964. The hospital had just purchased the machine, along with a cardioverter, as part of an expansion. The two pieces of equipment cost $15,000, plus the cost of creating a specially shielded room for the EEG device.

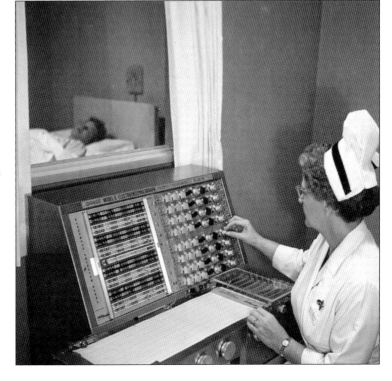

Nurses Bertha Wilkinson (left) and Margaret Bly learn how to set up an oxygen tent at Winter Park Memorial Hospital in September 1962. They participated in a three-week training session intended as a refresher for registered nurses who had been out of the profession for an extended period. Classes were held five days a week for four hours.

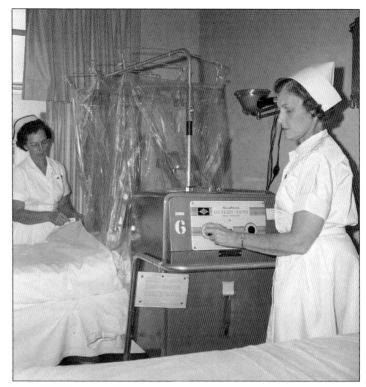

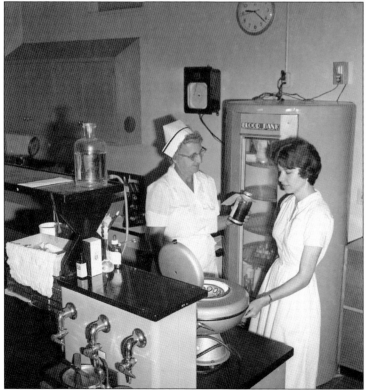

Mimi Cook, a nurse at Winter Park Memorial Hospital, receives instruction from Mary Best, a laboratory technician, during training sessions held in September 1962. Nurses also gained knowledge about using sterilizer machines, infant resuscitators, and Gomco suction devices. Mary Harris, director of service training, oversaw the sessions, along with Leon Benet-Alder, a hospital administrator.

Workers remove oak trees from a center island on E. Morse Boulevard in June 1963, the first step in an $85,000 paving and drainage project. City leaders expressed regret over removing the trees, but engineers said it was necessary so that a large drainage line could be buried under the center of the road. The Lincoln Apartments, which date to 1925, are at left.

Nine

CIVIC ORGANIZATIONS

Jim Barnhart (left), employee co-chairman, celebrates as Florida Gas Co. reaches its fundraising goal for the annual Community Chest campaign in October 1963, raising $6,163.92. Employees donated an average of $20 to reach the 100 percent mark for the fifth straight year. Joining Barnhart were co-chairman Les Gibson (right) and Gen. T.J. DuBose, general chairman of the Winter Park Community Chest.

Orange County Cancer Crusade opened a Winter Park office in March 1964 at 325 Park Avenue South, near the Park Plaza Hotel. Shown setting up the office, from left to right, are Henry Land, the county chairman; Bob Keezel, special gifts chairman for Winter Park–Maitland; and Mrs. Dan Hunter, the residential chairwoman.

Rollins College president Hugh McKean (second from left) talks to members of the Junior Chamber of Commerce in November 1963 after addressing the organization about little-known aspects of the college and its students. With McKean are, from left to right, Orlando Jaycees president Bob Crandall, Winter Park Jaycees president Bob Keezel, and first vice president Jim Mitchell.

Winter Park Junior Chamber of Commerce president Bob Keezel gets acquainted with a new Plymouth Fury provided in September 1963 for the club's use by A.P. Clark Motors of Orlando. It was the first time a dealership had offered a vehicle for the long-term use of the Jaycees.

Bob Milburn (left), president of the Orlando Lions Club, and Bill Roof, president of the Winter Park Lions Club, display some of the 50 paintings to be auctioned off in an event at the Winter Park Mall in December 1964. The paintings were donated by the Central Florida chapter of the American Artists Professional League.

Members of the Winter Park Exchange Club, including club president Sidney Ward (left), pose in December 1962. The local chapter of a national civic organization received its charter that year. The club provided a college scholarship each year to a high school senior involved with the Winter Park Youth Center.

Harold Hunt (left) hands over command of Winter Park Memorial American Legion Post 112 to Ben K. Armstrong (right) in a ceremony in June 1963. Ralph A. Johnson, state adjutant, served as installing officer. The post held an annual Memorial Day ceremony at Palm Cemetery, placing flags at the headstones of veterans.

Officers from the Does of the Winter Park Elks Club pose in January 1963. Virginia Lockhart (first row, center) was elected president. The club organized an annual blood drive, collected toys for children in need, and sponsored obedience classes for dogs. Many of the city's most prominent citizens were members of the club, which had its lodge at 420 South Orlando Avenue.

Congressman-elect and former Winter Park mayor Edward Gurney addresses a joint gathering of Winter Park and Maitland civic groups in December 1962. Gurney was receiving so many requests from civic organizations that he could not honor all of them, a spokesman for the Winter Park Rotary Club said. That club organized a combined meeting of nine groups so that all could hear Gurney speak.

Members of the Winter Park Junior Chamber of Commerce perform a safety check on a vehicle in 1964. The Jaycees provided the free service for one day, conducting a 10-point inspection of vehicles for local residents at the Aloma and Hollieanna Shopping Centers. It was part of the annual National Vehicle Safety Check for Communities, sponsored by the Auto Industries Highway Safety Committee and *Look* magazine.

Ten

RECREATION

Square dancers cover the floor at the Azalea Lane Recreation Center in the early 1960s. The Pioneer Square Dance Club regularly convened on Thursday nights, with Helen Everett and Eric Sohn serving as instructors and callers. The recreation center is still in use, offering meeting rooms rented for weddings, baby showers, dance classes, and birthday parties.

Spectators watch a baseball game at Rollins College's Harper-Shepherd Field in this undated photograph. Local merchants James E. Harper and F.W. Shepherd built the stadium at the corner of Aragon and Orange Avenues in the 1920s and donated it to the city, which gave possession to the college in 1934. Rollins demolished the stands in the 1980s to build Alfond Stadium at the same site.

The Lake Island Recreation Center opened in October 1963 at 450 Harper Street. The project included the digging of a seven-acre artificial lake. The city spent $55,000 on the construction of a multi-purpose building on the 26-acre tract. Architect Fred Owles designed the building, which is still in use.

The Winter Park Youth Center, which opened in 1961 at 2005 Mizell Avenue, hosted a range of activities, including dances, billiards, and ping pong, as well as classes in bridge, knitting, cosmetics, modeling, and hair-styling. The center featured a jukebox with records donated by Bill Baer, the owner of a television store, and a piano donated by Streep's Music.

A participant in the annual Winter Park Fish-A-Thon, sponsored by the Civitan Club, ends up with a reptile on his hook in this undated photograph. Children competed to see what they could catch from Lake Chelton, with prizes awarded for the largest fish, as measured by Civitan Club members, and the most fish landed.

A girl taking part in the annual Winter Park Fish-A-Thon opts to let a more experienced angler handle the baiting of her hook with a worm. The Civitan Club sponsored the event, usually held during the summer at Lake Chelton. The club awarded the most successful young angler a rod-and-reel set.

White and Black children swim together in the West Side Pool in June 1963. The only city-owned pool at the time became integrated when five white children entered the dressing rooms and the water at the previously "all-Negro" facility, the *Orlando Sentinel* reported. Police chief Carl D. Buchanan approached all the white children to ask if they had permission from their parents to be there.

A boy leaps from the high dive at West Side Pool in June 1963. The *Orlando Sentinel* covered the racial integration of the city-owned pool as five white children visited the facility, previously used only by Black residents. The white children, ages 6 to 10, mixed with the Black children with no incidents, the newspaper reported.

Jeannie Britt (left) and Dave Rowland display their diving skills at the season opening of the city's Olympic-sized swimming pool in April 1963. The event, marking the second year of operations for the pool, drew a large crowd. The private Winter Park Recreation Association contributed about $125,000 to help finance the project.

Children frolic in the West Side Pool in 1963. Five white children joined a group of Black children for an afternoon swim, marking the first time the city-owned facility had been racially integrated, the *Orlando Sentinel* reported.

A pair of lifeguards carry out their duties at the West Side Pool in the summer of 1963. The city-owned pool opened the previous year in the Hannibal Square area and was operated at that time by "Negro personnel" in the city's recreation department, according to the *Orlando Sentinel*. A fund donated $800 in 1963 to have lights installed at the pool in what is now Shady Park.

Jerri Carter (right) offers swimming instructions to a group of children at Dinky Dock on Lake Virginia in July 1963. The students taking a junior-senior lifesaving class were Robert Wray, Bruce Bowman, Kevin Cashin, Manny Heafner, Paul Brown, Pat Sloman, Mike Jones, and Ike Mann. Carter joined the city's recreation staff after graduating from Kansas State College. Countless Winter Park youths learned to swim by taking lessons from instructors at Dinky Dock.

Girls participate in a hopping race during a citywide Sports Day sponsored by the Winter Park Recreation Department in July 1962. Approximately 300 children took part in the competition, which included 13 events staged over two days. Kids from the Lakemont, Brookshire, and Azalea Lane recreation areas vied for prizes.

Children play ping pong in an undated photograph. Winter Park's parks and recreation department provided summer programs at nine locations in the early 1960s, with ping pong offered at Webster School, Glenridge School, and Brookshire School. Programs also promised softball, baseball, arts and crafts, checkers, hopscotch, swimming, tennis, and pet shows.

Boys practice to compete in a race that requires them to hold balls between their knees as they hop across a field. The contest was part of the citywide Sports Day sponsored by the Winter Park Recreation Department in July 1962. Children from the Lakemont, Brookshire, Glenridge, and Azalea Lane recreation areas competed in a series of events to win prizes.

Children take a break from participating in the beginners' class at the Winter Park Swim Club in August 1963. More than 700 youngsters joined the program that summer in the pool on Cady Way. The pool opened earlier that year and was operated by the nonprofit club. Standing are instructor Val Neeleman and assistant Jim Matteson.

Girls compete in a wheelbarrow race during the Sports Day event in July 1962. The city's recreation department closed all the playgrounds for the gathering at Ward Park. The competition included such events as a 50-yard dash, paper races, sack races, a softball throw, and an obstacle course. Prizes were awarded to the top four finishers in each category.

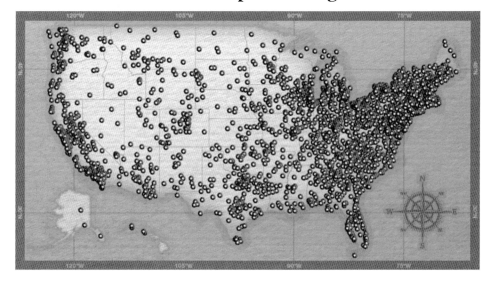